DO WHAT MAKES YOUR SOUL SHINE

summersdale

DO WHAT MAKES YOUR SOUL SHINE

An Hachette UK Company
www.hachette.co.uk

Summersdale Publishers Ltd
Part of Octopus Publishing Group Limited
Carmelite House
50 Victoria Embankment
LONDON
EC4Y 0DZ
UK

www.summersdale.com

Printed and bound in Malta

ISBN: 978-1-78783-011-0

Substantial discounts on bulk quantities of Summersdale books are available to corporations, professional associations and other organizations. For details contact general enquiries: telephone: +44 (0) 1243 771107 or email: enquiries@summersdale.com.

TO...................

FROM................

You have to be unique,
and different, and shine
in your own way.

LADY GAGA

FIND OUT WHO
YOU ARE AND BE
THAT PERSON...
FIND THAT TRUTH
AND EVERYTHING
ELSE WILL COME.

ELLEN DeGENERES

Everyone
zigs,
so zag

TODAY YOU ARE
YOU, THAT IS
TRUER THAN TRUE.
THERE IS NO ONE
ALIVE THAT IS
YOUER THAN YOU.

DR SEUSS

All we have to decide is what to do with the time that is given to us.

J. R. R. TOLKIEN

Live boldly. Push
yourself.
Don't settle.

JOJO MOYES

We cannot change the cards we are dealt, just how we play the hand.

RANDY PAUSCH

YOU CAN, YOU
SHOULD, AND IF
YOU'RE BRAVE
ENOUGH TO
START, YOU WILL.

Stephen King

GO AFTER YOUR DREAMS,
DON'T BE AFRAID TO
PUSH THE BOUNDARIES.
AND LAUGH A LOT –
IT'S GOOD FOR YOU!

PAULA RADCLIFFE

*If you don't
live your life, then
who will?*

RIHANNA

The formula of happiness and
success is just being actually
yourself, in the most vivid
possible way you can.

MERYL STREEP

Why not
you?

The art of being happy lies
in the power of extracting
happiness from common things.

HENRY WARD BEECHER

WHEN YOU
BECOME THE IMAGE
OF YOUR OWN
IMAGINATION,
IT'S THE MOST
POWERFUL THING
YOU COULD
EVER DO.

RuPAUL

I finally figured out the only reason to be alive is to enjoy it.

RITA MAE BROWN

Be brave
enough to be
your true self.

QUEEN LATIFAH

Practice any art... no matter
how well or how badly, not to
get money or fame, but to
experience becoming, to find
out what's inside you, and
to make your soul grow.

KURT VONNEGUT

NEVER DULL
YOUR SHINE FOR
SOMEBODY ELSE.

TYRA BANKS

Be your own

sunshine

If my mind can conceive it, and my heart can believe it – then I can achieve it.

JESSE JACKSON

FOLLOW
YOUR DREAMS.
THEY KNOW
THE WAY.

KOBI YAMADA

STAY STRONG
AND BE
YOURSELF!
IT'S THE BEST
THING YOU
CAN BE.

Cara Delevingne

DON'T COMPARE YOUR *rehearsal* WITH SOMEONE ELSE'S *final performance*

I DON'T KNOW WHERE I'M GOING FROM HERE, BUT I PROMISE IT WON'T BE BORING.

DAVID BOWIE

Make life
positively

you-shaped

You will
be fierce.
You will
be fearless.

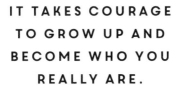

IT TAKES COURAGE
TO GROW UP AND
BECOME WHO YOU
REALLY ARE.

E. E. CUMMINGS

What gives you pleasure
and joy? Let those be the
things that lead you
forward in life.

JULIANNE MOORE

Motivation is when your dreams put on work clothes.

BENJAMIN FRANKLIN

Be sure
to take
enough
Vitamin
Me

I THINK WE CAN ALL
ACTUALLY BE MORE
SUPERHUMAN THAN
WE THINK WE CAN.

EDDIE IZZARD

YOU'LL NEVER FIND PEACE OF MIND UNTIL YOU LISTEN TO YOUR HEART.

George Michael

It's what
you do
each day
that
matters

The time is now.
Stop hitting
the snooze button
on your life.

MEL ROBBINS

The question isn't
who's going to let me;
it's who's going to
stop me.

AYN RAND

Follow your dreams like a satnav

If opportunity doesn't knock, build a door.

MILTON BERLE

YOU'RE THE STAR OF

The You

Show;

GO FOR AN EMMY

There are multiple sides to
all of us. Who we are – and
who we might be if we
follow our dreams.

MILEY CYRUS

TRUE HAPPINESS
COMES FROM THE JOY
OF DEEDS WELL DONE,
THE ZEST OF CREATING
THINGS NEW.

ANTOINE DE SAINT-EXUPÉRY

BE BRAVE
ENOUGH
TO LIVE
CREATIVELY...
WHAT YOU
DISCOVER
WILL BE
WONDERFUL:
YOURSELF.

ALAN ALDA

Creativity is contagious. Pass it on.

EUGENE RAUDSEPP

Listen to your heart above all other voices.

MARTA KAGAN

I THINK IT'S VERY
IMPORTANT TO DO
THINGS THE WAY YOU
WANT TO DO THEM AND
BE TRUE TO YOURSELF,
YOUR OWN GOALS, AND
YOUR OWN IDEALS.

ELISABETH MOSS

Accept who you
are; and revel
in it.

MITCH ALBOM

Life shrinks or expands in proportion to one's courage.

ANAÏS NIN

I WILL NO LONGER
COMPARE MY PATH
TO OTHERS, I REFUSE
TO DO A DISSERVICE
TO MY LIFE.

RUPI KAUR

Do your thing and don't care if they like it.

TINA FEY

Sing
your
own
song

Don't you ever let a soul
in the world tell you
that you can't be
exactly who you are.

LADY GAGA

IF YOU ASK ME
WHAT I CAME
INTO THIS LIFE TO
DO, I WILL TELL
YOU: I CAME TO
LIVE OUT LOUD.

ÉMILE ZOLA

IF YOU WORK
REALLY HARD,
AND YOU'RE
KIND, AMAZING
THINGS WILL
HAPPEN.

Conan O'Brien

Every now and again,
stop to
remind
yourself
how great
you are

You are never too old to
set another goal or to
dream a new dream.

LES BROWN

Throw caution to the wind and just do it.

CARRIE UNDERWOOD

LOVE CHALLENGES,
BE INTRIGUED BY
MISTAKES, ENJOY
EFFORT AND KEEP
ON LEARNING.

CAROL DWECK

VERA WANG started considering *fashion design at* 40... it's never too late

If you give people a chance, they shine.

BILLY CONNOLLY

Trust yourself.
You know more than
you think you do.

BENJAMIN SPOCK

IF YOU CAN DO WHAT
YOU DO BEST AND
BE HAPPY, YOU ARE
FURTHER ALONG IN LIFE
THAN MOST PEOPLE.

LEONARDO DiCAPRIO

Psst...
normal
isn't really
even a
thing

FIND SOMETHING
YOU'RE PASSIONATE
ABOUT AND KEEP
TREMENDOUSLY
INTERESTED IN IT.

JULIA CHILD

Change will not come
if we wait for some other person
or some other time. We are the ones
we've been waiting for.

BARACK OBAMA

We are
all of us stars,
and we deserve
to twinkle.

MARILYN MONROE

There's only one you, so cherish every quirk

IT IS NEVER
TOO LATE TO
BE WHAT YOU
MIGHT HAVE
BEEN.

Adelaide Anne Procter

Those who don't believe in
magic will never find it.

ROALD DAHL

Be yourself;
everyone else
is already taken.

ANONYMOUS

TELL ME, WHAT IS IT
YOU PLAN TO DO WITH
YOUR ONE WILD AND
PRECIOUS LIFE?

MARY OLIVER

It's okay to have butterflies in
your stomach. Just get them
to fly in formation.

ROB GILBERT

BELIEVE IN YOURSELF AND YOU CAN ACHIEVE GREATNESS IN YOUR LIFE.

Judy Blume

If you don't
love yourself, how
in the hell you gonna
love somebody else?

RuPAUL

Be happy.
It's one way
of being wise.

COLETTE

*Play
like you
never
grew up*

I PROMISE YOU
THAT EACH AND
EVERY ONE OF
YOU IS MADE
TO BE WHO
YOU ARE.

SELENA GOMEZ

ACT AS IF
WHAT YOU
DO MAKES A
DIFFERENCE.
IT DOES.

William James

Do.
Not.
Feed.
The.
Trolls.

The scariest moment is
always just before
you start.

STEPHEN KING

THE ONES WHO FEEL
LIKE THEY DON'T HAVE
A PLACE... YOU GOT
IT. JUST BE YOU.

MICHELLE VISAGE

Your victory is right around the corner. Never give up.

NICKI MINAJ

If cats don't

follow

rules,

WHY SHOULD YOU?

IF YOU TRULY POUR
YOUR HEART INTO
WHAT YOU BELIEVE IN...
AMAZING THINGS CAN
AND WILL HAPPEN.

EMMA WATSON

Ride the energy of your own unique spirit.

GABRIELLE ROTH

PROBLEMS ARE
NOT STOP SIGNS.
THEY ARE
GUIDELINES.

ROBERT H. SCHULLER

Be yourself.
The world worships
the original.

INGRID BERGMAN

If you're presenting yourself
with confidence, you can pull
off pretty much anything.

KATY PERRY

Don't let anyone

dull your sparkle

Whatever you can do or
dream you can, begin it.
Boldness has genius,
power and magic in it.

JOHANN WOLFGANG von GOETHE

I DON'T CARE
WHAT ANYBODY
SAYS; I LIKE
DOING IT, AND
IT'S WHAT I SHALL
CONTINUE TO DO.

DAVID BOWIE

Do something wonderful. People may imitate it.

ALBERT SCHWEITZER

DON'T ASK WHAT THE
WORLD NEEDS. ASK
WHAT MAKES YOU COME
ALIVE, AND GO DO IT.
BECAUSE WHAT THE
WORLD NEEDS IS
PEOPLE WHO HAVE
COME ALIVE.

BRENÉ BROWN

THERE IS A
FOUNTAIN OF
YOUTH: IT IS
YOUR MIND,
YOUR TALENTS,
THE CREATIVITY
YOU BRING TO
YOUR LIFE.

SOPHIA LOREN

Just be yourself, there is no one better.

TAYLOR SWIFT

BELIEVE YOU
CAN AND YOU'RE
HALFWAY THERE.

THEODORE ROOSEVELT

WHEN YOU
DO THINGS FROM
YOUR SOUL YOU FEEL
A RIVER MOVING
IN YOU, A JOY.

RUMI

Tell your story; the world is listening

Whatever you are, be a good one.

WILLIAM MAKEPEACE
THACKERAY

Go as far as you can see;
when you get there, you'll
be able to see further.

THOMAS CARLYLE

Every artist was first an amateur.

RALPH WALDO EMERSON

CHANGE YOUR
LIFE TODAY.
DON'T GAMBLE
ON THE FUTURE,
ACT NOW,
WITHOUT DELAY.

SIMONE DE BEAUVOIR

FIND OUT
WHO YOU ARE
AND DO IT
ON PURPOSE.

DOLLY PARTON

Once we believe in ourselves,
we can risk curiosity, wonder,
spontaneous delight or any
experience that reveals
the human spirit.

E. E. CUMMINGS

IF YOU HAVE GOOD
THOUGHTS THEY WILL
SHINE OUT OF YOUR
FACE LIKE SUNBEAMS
AND YOU WILL ALWAYS
LOOK LOVELY.

ROALD DAHL

Nothing can dim the light which shines from within.

MAYA ANGELOU

Crazy
ideas
make
amazing
lives

Follow your own fascination,
obsessions, and compulsions.
Trust them. Create whatever causes
a revolution in your heart.

ELIZABETH GILBERT

The most
important kind
of freedom is to
be what you
really are.

JIM MORRISON

Haters gonna hate; drown them out with joy

Loving what you do is the secret to everything.

JULIA ROBERTS

THE BIGGEST
ADVENTURE YOU CAN
TAKE IS TO LIVE THE LIFE
OF YOUR DREAMS.

OPRAH WINFREY

IT WILL NEVER BE
PERFECT, BUT PERFECT
IS OVERRATED.
PERFECT IS BORING.

TINA FEY

Weird is
beautiful

YOUR SOUL IS
ALL THAT YOU
POSSESS. TAKE IT
IN HAND AND MAKE
SOMETHING OF IT!

MARTIN H. FISCHER

The
world
loves you
just the
way you
are

You don't have to wait to be confident. Just do it and eventually the confidence will follow.

CARRIE FISHER

Follow
your inner
moonlight;
don't hide
the madness.

ALLEN GINSBERG

THE IMPORTANT THING
FOR YOU IS TO BE
ALERT, TO QUESTION,
TO FIND OUT, SO THAT
YOUR OWN INITIATIVE
MAY BE AWAKENED.

BRUCE LEE

WHEN YOU'RE
TRUE TO WHO YOU
ARE, AMAZING
THINGS HAPPEN.

Deborah Norville

Light tomorrow
with today!

ELIZABETH BARRETT BROWNING

SOME PEOPLE
SAY YOU ARE
GOING THE
WRONG WAY,
WHEN IT'S SIMPLY
A WAY OF
YOUR OWN.

ANGELINA JOLIE

I don't think limits.

USAIN BOLT

AS SOON AS YOU START
TO PURSUE A DREAM,
YOUR LIFE WAKES
UP AND EVERYTHING
HAS MEANING.

BARBARA SHER

WE HAVE TO DARE
TO BE OURSELVES,
HOWEVER
FRIGHTENING OR
STRANGE THAT SELF
MAY PROVE TO BE.

MAY SARTON

Doing what you love
is freedom. Loving what
you do is happiness.

LANA DEL REY

The
world
can't wait
to meet
you

I DON'T WANT OTHER
PEOPLE TO DECIDE WHO
I AM. I WANT TO DECIDE
THAT FOR MYSELF.

EMMA WATSON

Do what you were born to do. You have to trust yourself.

BEYONCÉ

YOU EITHER WALK
INSIDE YOUR STORY
AND OWN IT OR YOU
STAND OUTSIDE YOUR
STORY AND HUSTLE FOR
YOUR WORTHINESS.

BRENÉ BROWN

YOU'RE PERFECT
WHEN YOU'RE
COMFORTABLE
BEING YOURSELF.

ANSEL ELGORT

You have to rely on
whatever sparks
you have inside.

LISA KLEYPAS

If you're interested in finding out more about our books, find us on Facebook at **Summersdale Publishers** and follow us on Twitter at **@Summersdale**.

www.summersdale.com

Image credits

pp.1, 4, 5, 11, 12, 18, 20, 23, 25, 36, 38, 43, 44, 46, 50, 53, 63, 67, 76, 80, 84, 90, 94, 100, 103, 105, 106, 113, 118, 121, 129, 131, 138, 139, 144, 145, 148, 151, 156, 158, 159 – stars © Vdant85/Shutterstock.com

pp.3, 6, 35, 51, 60, 75, 95, 115, 134, 153 – stars © Alenka Karabanova/Shutterstock.com

pp.7, 39, 47, 55, 62, 74, 78, 89, 93, 116, 128, 132, 140, 152 – sparkles © Alex Gorka/Shutterstock.com

pp.9, 12, 16, 22, 28, 37, 45, 48, 57, 59, 72, 87, 96, 102, 117, 127, 130, 154 – circle design © MaddyZ/Shutterstock.com

pp.10, 24, 34, 42, 54, 61, 68, 71, 77, 82, 88, 99, 107, 111, 119, 133, 141, 147 – rays © Murvin/Shutterstock.com

pp.15, 31, 49, 58, 66, 70, 85, 97, 104, 112, 120 – stars © Giamportone/Shutterstock.com

pp.18, 27, 33, 81, 136 – rays © MG Drachal/Shutterstock.com